STRUGGLE AND CONTEMPLATION

STRUGGLE AND CONTEMPLATION

Journal 1970–2

BROTHER ROGER
Prior of Taizé

A Crossroad Book

THE SEABURY PRESS · NEW YORK

The Seabury Press
815 Second Avenue
New York, N.Y. 10017

Originally published as *Lutte et contemplation*
Copyright © 1973 by Les Presses de Taizé
English translation © 1974 by Les Presses de Taizé

LIBRARY OF CONGRESS CATALOGING IN
PUBLICATION DATA

Schutz, Roger.
  Struggle and contemplation: journal, 1970-2

  "A Crossroad book."
  Translation of Lutte et contemplation.
  1. Schutz, Roger.   2. Contemplation.   I. Title.
BR1725.S39A2813   282'.092'4 [B]   73-13954
ISBN 0-8164-2106-4

Printed in the United States of America

for
Felix Machado and
Cedric Lobo

CONTENTS

STRUGGLE AND CONTEMPLATION

STRUGGLE AND CONTEMPLATION

At the present time, no Christian can afford to lag behind in the rearguard of mankind, where there is so much useless strife. He must at all costs avoid becoming bogged down.

In the struggle for the voice of the voiceless to be heard, for the liberation of every person, the Christian finds his place—in the very front line.

And at the same time the Christian, even though he be plunged in God's silence, senses an underlying truth: this struggle for and with others finds its source in another struggle that is more and more etched in his deepest self, at that point in which no two people are quite alike. There he touches the gates of contemplation.

Struggle, contemplation: two poles between which we are somehow to situate our whole existence?

14 May 1970

Setting out, not knowing where we shall be led . . . six weeks now since the announcement of the Council of Youth. We have cut out moorings. Who knows, perhaps we and the young people will be able to strike out together and join with a very great number of men throughout the world.

15 May

The fascination of the sky, grey or dazzling, is with me as soon as I wake. It is something that is a dominant characteristic of many people who were born in the country. Rapidly rise to see what the weather is like. Light rain has dampened the ground. The trees on the terrace are gleaming under the cool rain. The lemon-balm is in bud, about to burst open. The sky is low but the earth sings.

16 May

What adventures have we embarked on? The preparation of the Council of Youth is bound to be a long march through a wilderness. The festival of the paschal mystery presupposes an inner combat that could be overwhelming for us at times. 'The heart that suffers redeems itself and begins to live anew' (Unamuno). That same festival leads to a struggle in company with men who are oppressed: it would soon wear out if we tried to live it for ourselves alone.

17 May

Could the call to reconciliation ever incite passivity or life without striving? No, the Gospel has never led to tranquility. Being reconciled with oneself, as with others, presupposes that we are ready to accept tensions and struggles. By neutralizing or fleeing situations of crisis, vital energy is destroyed. Passing through crises, seeing 'beyond . . .', is a path that takes us far.

18 May

Pinned to my wall are these words from the Cuban writer José Marti: 'Cuando otros lloran sangre, ¿qué derecho tengo yo para llorar lágrimas?' (When others are weeping blood, what right have I to weep tears?)

19 May

Very many young people, involved in struggles for greater justice, are experiencing discouragement. Buoyed up in recent years by a tremendous hope, many of them are now victims of bitterness or scepticism, both of them forms of self-destruction. In the presence of this kind of inner downfall, how can we communicate any optimism? There is a new element: we are capable, believers and non-believers together, of a common creation.

20 May

To follow Christ . . . becomes, in our consumer society, something heroic.

21 May

The full moon bathes the valley with peaceful light. In recent nights, when everyone is asleep, I have gone walking on the path leading to the hermitages. Just now, on the way back, I thought: in a century's time others will make similar walks in the night. I can imagine nothing about them, but the ground and the filtred light will be the same. Will the same searching lie in them?

24 May

Visit from Dom Helder Camara. He arrives with the challenge: 'Roger, I fear your death for the community.' Not at all expecting such words, I assure him that there is nothing to fear.

A little later, Dom Helder tells how happy he was to hear of the announcement of the Council of Youth, and adds, 'When I learned who had announced it, I thought, "Yes, Roger could"'.

I ask him what he thinks most important for young Europeans. He points to the long table ready under the trees to welcome the Portuguese immigrants invited here to meet him:

In the countries of Europe there are vast islands of poverty. The Third World is also in your midst, with the poor you have in Europe, the immigrants who come seeking work; they are more or less well received and their living conditions are often wretched. In Europe you often talk a lot about the development of the Third World, but do not forget your own development problems. In not working for a solution here, you give support to the imbalance of misery existing in our countries.

Dom Helder! Eight years have passed since we first discovered one another. Never a shadow in our friendship: a rare friendship, with a man of many faces, like quicksilver, full of warmth in his vivid language and his gestures.

I remember how in Rome, when he came to share a meal with us, he would draw a paper from his pocket, put on his glasses, and read us something of the speech that he was currently preparing. At such moments he became another man—one who intends to convince, to communicate some basic idea. I think that every address he gave during the Council was first read out at our dining-table.

25 May

Community living makes it possible to acquire culture from one another. Simply by being interested in the work of one's brothers, there is no telling the treasures available in easy reach. Being enriched by a process of osmosis!

26 May

A new discovery of our district: unknown landscapes just beyond the garden walls. Now that a gateway has been pierced, as we have always wished, it is at last possible to leave the house and walk northwards along the hill in solitude, even though there may be much activity close by.

27 May

The forecasts of doom arising from the pollution of air or water are intolerable. Affluent countries have affluent problems! Modern technology will find the necessary solutions. Do not try to divert our energies to bother about that. It results in us seeking our own selves and there are better things to be done.

2 June

Why are incompatibilities so common between exceptional people? Some explain it by a form of rivalry and its consequence: the inability to be oneself. A jealous man dares not believe that he is complementary to the other; he prefers to copy him. Such imitations are invariably caricatures.

3 June

For love, man does not have at his disposal a particularly wide range of impulses. He employs the same flows of affection for human love or for the love of Christ.

4 June

Christ understands everything in man. Can I too, in every situation, understand everything? Not approving of sin, when man ensnares man, but grasping all the reasons why. Yes, as far as that.

6 June

It has often been protestant pastors who have tried to discourage us from our life commitments. Of course, these commitments were abolished at the Reformation. When certain Catholic Religious abandon their promises, these pastors betray a reaction: 'The Reformation was right!'

They condemn the ecumenism of 'return to the fold' that some Catholics profess, and yet they practise an ecumenism that says 'come and be like us'. What is the distinction? Luckily there are other pastors whose generosity knows no bounds.

9 June

I wonder why, especially in days of relaxation, my mind runs into a riot of architectural planning. My great-grandmother, whom I love without having known—my sisters and my mother have often told me about her—used to fall asleep reorganizing the interior decoration of houses. Transferred to a man's mentality, this means building and constructing.

Would she have had the same need for something to pass the time if she had not been left a widow so early? Her husband was a great traveller. He often used to cross the Atlantic in the clippers. Brought down by tuberculosis, he left her with two daughters and two sons. The latter were both to die of the same disease, one at five, the other at twenty.

Perhaps it was these misfortunes that drove her in her distress to imagine so many ways of arranging the house? So what is it for me? Why am I incapable of living somewhere without imagining changes to be made? I estimate distances, how to demolish, and, always, how to simplify. It is the same when I read a novel: irresistibly I begin to rewrite it. Often what I read simply provides the outline for a different novel.

11 June

Here in the house we have abolished offices. They give work too much solemnity and make too much of a cult of it. So we should have nothing but what is essential for communication.

15 June

Freedom has a high price. Recently, with much generosity, certain church officials wished to show their support by offering us the wherewithal to pay for many of the journeys which young people are making to visit one another throughout the world. We preferred to refuse these gifts, rather than risk losing something of our freedom.

22 June

When it comes to getting married, some people decide very rapidly. Others opt equally rapidly for celibacy. Is there any reason to think that such people are more mistaken than others who spend a long time weighing everything but who have, later, to admit that their evolution has gone in directions which they would never have thought possible?

A YES THAT REMAINS YES

Once again I hear a middle-aged man tell me things that have become commonplace: 'When I married, I was so conditioned that I was unable to stand back and see things clearly. Now, I have found the woman of my life.' Of course, at twenty-three he was not totally clear sighted. But at what age will he be?

Of necessity, to make one choice excludes for ever certain other options. Otherwise we become wanderers: ready to say yes, but only for the moment, without continuity.

The 'yes' of marriage—like that of celibacy for the Gospel—sets us on the crest of a ridge, because it involves the total person: the body and all the inner resources of intelligence, sensitivity, affectivity, imagination.

The person who has pronounced such a 'yes', giving up any idea of looking back, says over and over to Christ, all through life, 'I trust you, I believe you on your word'. To await some kind of total lucidity before pronouncing a yes that is to remain yes could perhaps leave us with nothing but leftovers to offer?

This yes, once pronounced, becomes the pivot for a whole life of creativity, a column around which to twirl in freedom, a spring beside which to dance.

For such a person, moments will come when to be faithful no longer springs spontaneously from the heart: the 'yes' is a burden, accepted without love. Perhaps then, for just a while, the law may have to take control, as our guardian, until once more love springs forth.

Only for a while; there are those who set themselves under the law for their whole lives: but what a life, full of monotony and routine! Sooner or later everything grows rigid. Nothing is more disheartening than people frozen into the appearances of a vocation reduced to its sociological forms.

23 June

High summer, vast skies of light. The wind is rising. Darkness is falling across the valley from west to east.

I surprise myself by the unusual terms I use in writing to certain young South Americans. I know that their commitment in favour of man springs from love for Christ. Around them men, women, and children are barely conscious of being human persons. A daily nightmare. Oligarchies, often composed of Christians, stifle any capacity they may have for taking control of their fate.

I have never been more totally behind these young Christians, and I write to tell them so. They are preparing the day when they will take up arms to overthrow tyranny, but they are not searching for their own interests. When the time comes, they will be able to lay them aside again. They will refuse to enter into the process under which, the tyrant once overthrown, any means are justified in the strife to become leaders. I pray with them. Although I know that the Gospel in me contests the use of violence, I am in communion with them, since oppressive violence so marks the society in which they live.

24 June

Robert, as he is about to leave Lima for Cuba, sends me this text written by a young girl belonging to a group of Christian revolutionaries. A letter to contemplatives:

I am writing to those contemplatives who feel concerned by the suffering and the struggles of man today. In the name of all who are struggling, known or unknown, in the name of all those committed to building a new society, I ask you urgently not to give up your vocation. Find how to be totally attentive to men, sharing their searching, their successes and their failures, all their struggles. Live in the rhythm of men's joys and men's sorrows. But do not be afraid of doing so within what you have been called to. Of course, seek new forms. But do not reject what is fundamental in the call you have received from the Lord. The world has need of it, even though it may not realize it or explicitly say so.

25 June

Visit of a young bishop from northern Italy. The transparency of his heart gives us a hint of what a bishop in Italy will be like in the Church of the future. Those most capable of understanding the quite new vitality that is manifesting itself everywhere are also the most ill-used : people have no hesitation in profiting from their openness.

26 June

This afternoon Bernard, a young man from a near-by village, was ordained priest in the church at St Gengoux. Since time immemorial no one has been ordained in these parts. I recall the welcome I received from the priest of this same village thirty years ago, how from the first moment he gave me his trust. At that time his church was always practically empty—it seemed as though everything had been extinguished for ever. He too was giving help to political refugees. I live anew one of our first encounters : Emmanuel Mounier happened to be passing through Taizé and the two of us cycled over to see him. We were both enthralled : lost in this isolated corner, he was full of attention for all that was happening.

3 July

Engineers following a refresher course in information-processing share our supper. An atheist amongst them vigorously contests all that Christians believe. His scientific mind gauges everything by what he can know. At the end of the evening I tell him: 'The questions you have been asking are questions that a man living by the certainty of God also dares to keep asking himself during his life. This kind of questioning, part of our basic doubt, does not prevent us from constantly setting out from doubt towards belief'.

7 July

Some people, sensing timidity in others, immediately adopt an intimidating approach towards them. But surely it is better not to be feared, even though this may encourage pressuring or a kind of blackmailing, rather than try to adopt a distant attitude that only evokes an artificial respect?

8 July

We have just buried little Jean-Christophe Rémy, my sixty-seventh great-nephew. Why the death of this child? For us—unable to understand his death in any way— after a first attack of pitiful grief, a star has shone out in the darkness.

12 July

I am still amazed to see the constant floods of young people arriving on the hill. When I came to Taizé in 1940, I had no inkling of this. I used to say to my first brothers, 'We will stop at twelve brothers . . .'. Then, when crowds began to come, we longed to move away. It took lay people from the region to keep us here. But I would like to remain ignorant as to where we shall die.

15 July

Tiredness, loss of drive. Day, pass quickly! Days, pass quickly! Tiredness and indifference to Christ are the same.

Come to Christ in simple ways. Listen to yourself breathing: you share in a life. . . . Listen to the clock striking. . . . Listen to the wind in the lime-trees. . . .

18 July

Max and I went walking along the brow of the hill as far as Ameugny. All was enchanting. We walked, saying little. A stroll in shades of blue. To the north, the slopes above St Gengoux bursting with joy, yellow corn to warm the blues. Alfalfa just sprouting from the dry, cracked soil. A series of small fields yielding little—vines, potatoes, corn. Fullness of vast horizons dominated at this time of year by the song of skylarks.

23 July

Among the children beside me at the midday prayer is Maria de Fatima. A month ago she and her grandmother crossed the Portuguese frontier secretly. Her father was killed in Angola. She is often here beside me, praying with her face pressed to the floor.

26 July

In the post comes a post card of the front of a church illuminated in the night. On the back a message, 'Thank you for the night-light'. The child who wrote it was beside me with the other children for several days. Puzzling and uncommunicative. No response until one day, questioning him, I discovered that he was afraid of the dark. At the next service I gave him a night-light for his bedroom.

All the children close to me each day! If they only knew how much their waiting for Christ supports our own!

28 July

Four in the morning. Went out for a moment as I do almost every day at dawn. The star-studded sky is growing pale. A dim dawn begins to break. A month before at this hour the northern sky was transparent, clear green, then rapidly ablaze. Now autumn mists are already toning down much of the light's brilliance. In a few hours I shall again be taking the path along the hill as far as the church—the path I was walking along yesterday evening, pausing to breathe in the night—a burning eastern night. Today everything is gentle again. The distant views are light and peaceful. I am truly restored to the Burgundy that bore my mother's ancestors.

29 July

All these days, long talks with three young Latin Americans. Yesterday afternoon we found, only a few minutes away, an unknown and delicious path. I had not realized that the forester's lodge at Praye marked the start of a path through the thick woods. Age-old beech trees, carpets of russet leaves.

Pedro—a master thinker—is haunted by what response to give to the revolutionary movement. Carlos is tense, worried to think that the Church moves ahead in declarations; many words, with the same emptiness after as before. Victor listens. He will soon be back in his country. His desire is to bear a simple witness there, nothing more. He is preparing himself for that.

Pedro resumes:

Without places that offer the possibility of being immersed in a contemplative form of prayer for limited periods, how can we avoid being rapidly consumed by ideas? In Latin America, who will maintain a continuity at certain places where prayer opens towards a sense of eternity and where men of every tendency are given attention?

30 July

Have come up against strong resistance in recent days to the fact that South Americans have so big a place in the preparation for the Council of Youth.

An then yesterday I was told of a young black bishop here on the hill. I met him at noon, just before the common prayer. In a few moments I realize that it is an exceptional encounter. Yet we have said little. Several others are waiting their turn. We agree to eat together. And there I shall persuade him to spend a few days here.

In the evening we are together in my room. Suddenly he asks me to help him know himself better and, to that end, to question him, so that he may be a man of truth. I accept but intend the questioning to be reciprocal. 'Do not be afraid of crossing me', he says. I would not be capable of it.

2 *August*

Heat pouring down on the fields. But the nights are incomparably cool.

Started to read *Le lys dans la vallée*. I have not opened any work of Balzac since I was fifteen. My mind fills with recollections of long readings as a whole family. I see again Lily, the sister whose death came so prematurely, gathering us together during the autumn days in father's study and reading to the youngest of us a series of passages from Balzac.

How is it that I am carried back yet farther, to my early childhood, the years when my maternal grandmother played such a prominent role? I loved her for her calm dignity. She used to live somewhere in western Paris. Perhaps forgotten stories are the reason I look so poetically westwards and see there a kind of gate to Happiness (and I find myself writing the word with a capital H!)

During the years of my childhood, it was my grandmother who in my eyes represented all feminine understanding. I have often imagined scenes of high-topped trees bathed by the setting sun in the midst of vast meadows and there, sitting below the foliage, my grandmother and mother welcoming us. From them I learned to love vast farm houses. Apparently when I was still only a child I used to say how, one day, I would live in the country and welcome others. I would even plan programmes for the days, with much time reserved for reading aloud.

Late afternoon: nothing more serene than this moment at the end of a hot Sunday. The tireless music of a blow-fly. Quiet in my room. Windows shut because of the stifling heat outside. The shutters to the south closed as well. All the light enters through the northern window and there I sit to write.

I keep open the door giving onto the stairs of the *salle claire*, coolness comes flooding up from below.

3 August

The third conversation with Cipriano will remain etched within me. He tells of his fortnight of reflection here. And then he begins to insist that he wants to take what he has lived here in Taizé and transpose it to his home in Central America. I suggest that he should rather search how to enter into his country's life, without imitating anybody. And I conclude: 'Forget Taizé!' I am sad to have to speak thus, but we are about to part for good. The bells are ringing and it is important to find words that will be understood. Forget Taizé: forget us, his friends! It is an inhuman thing to ask—besides, will he be able to? . . . Similar conversations, one after another, are wearing.

4 August

For the second time today I am about to see a young worker-priest. I was preparing to meet somebody exhausted by struggles and I discover a quiet youth, master of himself, burning with the love that fills him. Clear blue eyes. His features, thickened by physical tiredness, crease at every smile. The face of a man who has bcome poor in company with those who are victims.

5 August

The young African bishop of a few days ago has returned after an absence. He wants to be called by his Christian name, Stanislas. He talks about his childhood, the love he has for his people. His father and mother were animists, he is a Christian of the first generation. He constantly refers, as a theologian, to Irenaeus: in the second century, he too was part of a newly-born Church.

The night is mild. The breeze passes straight through my room. A walk is calling me. In the deep of night or at the first light I shall go to consult the sky—what weather are we going to have?

DAWN AT NIGHT'S END

As a man grows older, he is less inclined to look for signs. He dares admit to himself that he is familiar with darkness.

In this realm, no one is privileged. Even psychologists and scholars of the highest order admit that they are at the first stammerings of their sciences, that they can only understand one outer layer of the human being.

To each one his night, but the darker the shadows become, the more a man discovers the delight of believing. Does belief not include consenting to our night? To refuse our night would be to seek a privilege. If we should see as in open day, to what purpose believe?

Advancing on a road without knowing where it leads, such a man believes without seeing. No fear of the shadows, they are lit from within.

Certainty solid as the rock: at a given moment the night is rent and dawn appears.

So let this dawning come, and one day our death, dawn of a life.

10 August

I was brought up in the old traditions, but listening to younger people and sharing in their private struggles rids me of certain reflexes of fear. Without these thousands of young people here on the hill, where would I be now, in spite of my desire to be open?

11 August

Christian women ensure continuities, keep up a living tradition, share with their children the essence of the Gospel. We men, with our eagerness to be up to date, to live God's today, to achieve something, are liable to tackle nothing but the immediate present; and—at times—with such fuss!

12 August

Martin brings me a drawing at the church with an inscription in childish writing: 'You will never be old.' I ask what he means. He explains: 'I shall be your servant and I will bring you food to eat.' This child here beside me, seven years old, alert and silent: 'I will bring you food to eat'—words that will console me for many days.

14 August

Below my window, two doves are perched motionless on the edge of the trough. The water is stale and they hesitate to wash in their usual fashion. But the day is heavy and they are drawn irresistibly towards this source of refreshment. They have been there now for a good while, although normally they are lively and nervous. As I write

I glance up to watch them, waiting motionless for the storm that refuses to break.

There is not enough time for observation and I begin to envy the poet. Obviously I do not intend to refuse the enormous pressures of existence which make themselves felt even here in my room day after day. But poetic creation is a way of freedom.

19 August

All my life I have dreaded the thought of signs that are too great for me. Until now we have been taken at our word. But today Raymond Oliver and his wife came to say goodbye after a stay of ten months at Taizé. Casually, he tells me something that he had not even mentioned to his wife:

On the evening of 16 August, during the prayer, we were all turned towards the sanctuary of the church. Looking up, he sees, a few yards away from the icon there, the form of a woman holding a child, in a strange light. He shuts his eyes several times, even asks his wife if she can see anything. The form remains visible until the end of the prayer, but he alone sees it. He supposes that it could be Mary with Jesus, but with his protestant background he is completely unaware of everything to do with the Virgin.

He had not even intended mentioning it this morning.

20 August

Man only creates by drawing on his poverty. I am well-placed to assert that today: it is exactly thirty years ago that I discovered Taizé.

2 September

Words noted by Elizabeth who has just left: 'If I look back over all the mistakes in my life, it seems that they can be summed up in this: at times I have left Christ in favour of other people, at times I have left other people aside in favour of Christ. I never realized that I had to leave myself aside'.

Giving others up in favour of Christ—washing one's hands of everything to do with men in the present day; or giving up Christ for others in order to be committed for greater justice. This kind of alternating tears apart and dislocates. Never Christ without men! Never men without Christ!

6 September

I have never been so impatient for winter to come. The wood fire to kindle each morning. Scanning the sky for all the effects of filtred light, the sunset skies, dizzying greatness.

Went walking in the meadows. Sheep have browsed the grass down to the bare earth. Beyond the hedges that keep off the north wind, the flock quietly pursues its slow way forward, paying no attention to my presence. Once I am surrounded on every side. These round, peaceful animals feed with surprising feverishness. Their panting breath blends in a single musical note, a cantilena.

11 September

Today my mother begins her ninety-first year. Where does she find her energy, her capacity to read, write, receive guests, remember faces even of the newest acquaintances? She has the solidity of her ancient Burgundian forebears.

20 September

Today, during the council of the community, we were speaking of the incomprehension that we shall have to face concerning certain realizations of the preparation of the Council of Youth. Any initiative is bound to provoke contrary forces. And we have only just begun.

22 September

To have opted for love: that choice opens in a man a wound from which he never recovers.

23 September

This morning, while I was still asleep, a thought came to me, so precise that I noted it down straight away: 'My friend, tell me at least where you live and I will tell you where I am. You will see, we are not so far apart.'

If words can come together this logically, even in sleep, why worry about what to say in public? The lips have simply to follow what is already composed within.

14 October

Lines from a young Latin American: 'My mind is still restless, worried, and despairing. With an immense hope I ask you to search with us: how to find a light, how to set a light within the Latin-American revolution to make it radical, dynamic, and aimed at lasting peace'.

30 October

Every day this week I have talked with a young Italian priest. Why does the trouble in the Church so undermine this man?

In him I have seen holiness from very close at hand. At times I could only say: 'Weep'. Once I even went to find a handkerchief for him in a drawer. Weep, because it is not possible to bear such a struggle alone in stony silence. Face to face with him, I have touched on what it can mean for a man to be abandoned. Persons of silence exist who radiate communion. The price they pay is high.

As the days went by, the face of Christ appeared to me in this priest whom struggles have so harrowed. The depth of his gaze could conceal nothing of his successive ordeals. He has shown me the heart of one of the greatest mysteries: the gift of a whole existence for other men, at the risk of losing all of oneself.

Before parting, after so many days of being close, I knelt for him to bless me. He had seen that I would not wish him to do likewise.

RESTORE TO PASTORS
A SPIRIT OF FESTIVAL

The present crisis of confidence in man strips away the identity of many who have consented to be priests. They are at a loss to know what use they can be. Where does the essence of their calling lie? I can see three specific features:

The man of priesthood sets out to find in Christ his first and basic love. He exposes his life, even gives it for those who are his.

Being the unbinder on earth of what is then at once unbound before Christ, he is also the man who sets free. He practises listening, sounding out the hidden depths of the human person. The older he grows, the more he learns to understand and restore to men their freedom.

And it is he who makes it possible for man to live by the paschal mystery in the eucharist.

How could those who respond to this calling live it out in isolation, without us? What can we do for them, with them? More than we dare think. Not leaving them to their solitude. Bringing them our trust. Seeking by their liberating ministry a heart that is poor, reconciled, unified by Jesus Christ. And, in so doing, restore to them 'the festive sound of joy and gladness'.

Some people say that there exist bad pastors. When that is so, better to remain silent. . . . How could we, who struggle in ourselves because of our own fragility and vulnerability, demand that others be supermen?

31 October

Unique sunset. Flaming landscape and between the flames piercings of gold and pale green.

1 November

I love my room, with its orange walls, the floor of wide pine planks and the ceiling of painted beams. Some of us have a larger room, others a smaller. Some sleep on a mattress laid on the floor and have nothing but a table and a cupboard; others prefer to have more colour around them. For each of us, once the door is shut, there awaits the same solitude. Of course, there is the kitchen where we find others around eleven in the evening, to talk and hear what is happening. Then each returns to his room and closes the door. Our yes to Christ for life means making this gesture every evening. Sometimes it costs. But this solitude is not to seek one's own self . . . as the years pass, it opens us to the unique reality, Christ our first love.

2 November

Waking up in the night, I read a few pages of Victor Chlosky's *Tolstoy*. As I put out the light, my mind remains fixed on Tolstoy and Yasnaya Polyana. To think that his daughter is still alive and could tell so much! Hour of joy given by the presence of a fascinating Russia!

3 November

Struck as a small child by all my parents' great worries, I used to make them mine and be tormented by them. I became aware of life, a large family, a father anxious about having to provide for everything. It was at that time, so as not to add to my parents' existing burdens, that I grew into the habit of not telling them of my own difficulties. And even now, afraid of overburdening my brothers with my preoccupations, I observe silences which must, in fact, be hard for them.

17 November

Days marked by the presence of a Mexican. In his view, the faithful Church is ever on the outskirts of society, contesting it, denouncing oppressive powers, the power of wealth, privileges. It sets itself in a situation of weakness. To interpret events it sees as those who are oppressed see.

20 November

Another Mexican at our table. I tell him how, three days ago, his place was occupied by a young revolutionary from his country. My brothers are astonished: so he was a revolutionary, that boy who in great simplicity shared with us his conviction: if the Mexican people were evangelized, it is thanks to the Virgin who in the sixteenth century appeared to a poor peasant. The likeness of the Virgin, with Indian features, left its imprint on the peasant's cloak and the attention of the masses has remained centred around that sign for the past four centuries.

21 November

Words of a little girl who lost her mother a few years ago: 'When you own a lot of things, you are rich, but when you do not have all that, perhaps you are rich in love'.

22 November

The past interests me less and less. What lies ahead I view in an optimistic light.

23 November

Woken in the night by noises: mice gallivanting more riotously than ever. I seem to feel the breath of one on my cheek. No, they have never been that bold. And suddenly I sense something on the blankets. I turn on the light, and see before me a huge sewer-rat. I leap out of bed, see that my wrist is scratched and bleeding. I realize that this is the daily lot of many of the badly housed.

24 November

A few years ago I talked with an economist, a non-believer, of conversations I was about to have with certain leading churchmen. He warned: 'Talks about money and power in the Church will crush you; people break against the wall of money.' Those talks took place and, as he said, they were a complete failure . . . but it does not mean that I am shattered.

25 November

Certainly accept that we are in a pre-revolutionary period, with criticism and conflict as expressions of relationship. But still have ways of setting things in an inner perspective when criticism resorts to polemical methods or threats. The Christian can never identify needful criticism with contempt for persons.

3 December

At Rome since Sunday. Yesterday Charles-Eugène, Bruno, and I decided to take the train for Eboli. The carriage is full of young people and women from southern Italy, each fascinated by the sound of his or her own voice. It is a matter of who can talk with most demonstrations. The train is going at full speed: the warm air billows in through the corridor windows.

Leaving the train, we find a car for hire that will take us up to the mountain villages; and before long we are in Eboli, where Carlo Levi, in one of his novels, shows how 'Christ stopped at Eboli'. Beyond, nothing but ruin and misery. We speed on along the foot of the mountain, through high-grown meadows. Roads lined with olive trees. Then the car plunges into a narrow, sunless gorge. And in a flash we see before us, perched on one side of the valley, the village of Campagna.

The car comes to a halt in a square, at the foot of a high, white palazzo. We continue on foot, climbing up and down narrow alley-ways filled with children.

In one vast room, lit through the open door, a man is weaving straw chair-seats. He tells us of his life. When it is cold, he lights a fire in one corner of the room. The smoke climbs up beneath the soot-stained vault and escapes through a hole. He claims to be old. When still in the prime of life, he spent seven years working in Germany. His eyes sparkle green. His toothless smile and drawn features can conceal nothing of the struggles making up his life. The more he tries to explain his existence here, the more I am struck by the inner fervour, the contemplative vigour that are his. No, Christ did not stop at Eboli: he continued up to Campagna, he is here and this man is, unconsciously, a sign of him. I want to tell him so, but something holds me back. For all the rest of the afternoon his face pursues me. Why did we not dare to tell him we were Christians, and that in his house we encountered the one we seek after?

At the village's highest point we join a crowd. Leaning against the walls of a house are wreaths interwoven with carnations, ready to be carried to the church. Women and children are entering and leaving the house of the deceased through the vaulted gateway. The women are visibly afflicted, one still has tears on the edge of her upper lip. Most are dressed for work, in aprons. A gleaming coffin emerges from the house. Only the men of the family follow the widower. The dignity of the sons is in tune with the respect of the crowd.

As we walk down we are invited, as we were on the way up, to enter various houses. We do not dare to, except for one tiny kitchen full of a dozen children. On the table a loaf three-quarters eaten. The excitement of the children as we pass.

Leaving Campagna, we drive on towards Valva. The hills are planted with ancient, towering oaks. Sometimes a huge pig attached to a tree scratches after the falling acorns. At other places there is an old man gathering more acorns along the edge of the road. We cross the valley. Before us rises the mountain. A land of old men clinging to the rocks. All is slowly dying. In one village the bell is tolling. Another funeral. We enter the church whose sanctuary is built out on a substructure, the foundations descending to the very foot of the ravine. In the church there is a little group gathered around the coffin: a father, his sons, a few women. In the street, all the doors are already shut. A youth is carrying wood. He invites us to enter. Before the flames on the hearth his young wife is stooping to stir the pasta. An old couple, and two tiny children. They suggest that we wait and eat.

At Valva, thick mists still reflect some glimmers of daylight. Two women are coming down the street bearing bundles on their heads. With them is a large peasant, ample and round, smiling broadly. When he speaks, there is no mistaking the cheerfulness of his tone. The women are laughing at the sight of a sheepskin sticking out from beneath his jacket. An old couple are watching us from a high-up terrace. They gesture to come up to their home— too small a house, the husband maintains. A bright room, a fire. His wife, broken with age, seems more like his mother. They insist on offering us coffee. The old man leads us behind a curtain so that we can see their large modern bed. Everything is gleaming and fresh, as he repeats, 'Too small'.

4 December

Yesterday Thomas rejoined us after a month in England. To celebrate his arrival we climbed to the top of the Pincio. The city is already plunged in shadow. Irresistibly our talk turns to Taizé.

One brother mentioned a comment made by my sister Geneviève about our first years at Taizé: 'It was a time of unbearable sadness.' It was wartime. The people we were housing were on the run, being hunted after. And then certain people in the district, anxious to be on the side of security, took measures against us which could have brought grave consequences. A written accusation was drawn up against Geneviève and the worst could happen.

It was at that time that I discovered what man is capable of towards man. I can locate the exact moment of that discovery. When I learned the inconceivable, I was at the foot of the wood. I returned up to the house and on the stairway beside my room I stopped, frozen with horror. I knew that I would never at any time seek to take revenge.

I write this twenty-four hours after having talked of it in order to unburden myself.

6 December

Morning alone. I read letters, almost all of them written by young people, a bath of life. In them I find the inner struggles of my own youth. But I also discern a refusal to settle down not at all customary thirty years ago.

7 December

Read once more a letter which Daniel sent to me at Rome some years ago. In it he tells of a dream he had :

We are in the Vatican, at the very top of a many-storied block, at a papal audience. The crowd fills the whole room and we are beside Paul VI. The Pope, consumed with worry, has collapsed on to a simple chair. Meanwhile a priest, apparently spokesman for the Holy Father, is addressing words to the crowd, against which the Pope attempts in vain to protest. At this moment you intervene, scandalized at this abuse of power, but not for long. We hear the cries of a group of pilgrims under whom the flooring which is quite rotten is giving way. In a moment, all the planking dissolves into dust. We and the Holy Father remain balanced on a beam until an obliging person places a ladder—too short but nonetheless effective—allowing us to climb down to the foot of the building, where we find a crowded market in progress.

And the brother adds this commentary to his dream: So I suppose that the situation in the Church worries us even in the depth of night. The Church, carefully hidden in us and around us . . . of no great appearance but within, what fire.

OUR COMMUNION, A BURNING FIRE

Thirsty for a real commitment in favour of man, many young people are searching how to communicate.

For young Christians, the word is communion. That calls for no very rigid framework: their predecessors in the 1950s and early 1960s were openly hostile towards the Church's institutions. The present generation tends not to care about them. They give little attention to reforms since they are demanding rebirths. Their instinctive confidence is towards individuals, living experience and men or women of communion. When denominational organizations go out of their way to involve young people, they find themselves accused of trying to recuperate the young for their own ends.

Many have a strong sense of being part of a human community of planetary dimensions, having a clear vision of the universal; many young people look for their fulfilment in a socialized society on a world-wide scale.

Certain people love Christ in isolation, without his body the Church. In their thinking, the Church has often already been replaced by a political universalism. I would worry little about that, were it not for the last prayer of Christ before his death: he asks that, as he is in communion with his Father, so a demanding communion of the same nature should exist among his followers. He has that final intuition: the credibility of Christians passes by way of the communion which binds them in a single body.

If Christians seek to be visibly in communion, this is not an end in itself, for a greater sense of ease or for greater power, but it is in order to be seen to be truthful by men around, in order to be able to offer to all men a place of communion where even non-believers can feel at ease, under no kind of constraint.

So I have never better understood what is at stake in the Church, and what lies at stake when it is rejected, or in those underlying struggles which are current in it.

Our communion, a fire kindled over the whole earth, burns us.

11 December

Very often, whatever we may think, our ordeals, failures, and standstills constitute a driving-force stimulating us to create—to such an extent that the impossible becomes the way towards the possible.

21 December

Return to Taizé. There I find lines written by a youth:

> To be free is knowing that you are in chains, and still setting out: knowing that you are going to fall, and still standing up. But it is hard. . . . Nonetheless I strive; I try to hang on and always end by falling back. It means fighting. I want to prepare the Council of Youth but I must have festival in myself to start with.

22 December

In Paris to pray before the mortal remains of Pastor Boegner. The coffin is exposed in his drawing room. Before closing it, his family placed in it his Bible and the Taizé office which he prayed daily.

Now at midday the light is dazzling. The houses are dominated by huge clouds. We take a taxi with an elderly woman driving. As we cross the Seine, we talk to her about the light. Today the days begin to grow longer. Wonder: a sky, decorated streets, all that can be read in people's faces.

28 December

The prisoners of the Burgos trial were today condemned to death. This evening I sent General Franco a telegram, prepared with various young people: 'In the name of human dignity, show mercy to the Burgos prisoners. In each man God is present. Do not wound the consciences of the young. With many of them we ask you this.'

29 December

Just before Christmas, three youths returned from Spain. They had been there for a month and they told their stories gravely. There are narratives which cause discouragement but not despair. Today, after the midday office, we shared a meal to celebrate their return. Festivity in the heart of struggle; and festivity around a meal. Tiny community poised in expectation, knowing the importance of a presence hidden in our midst. Before me flashed all the meals that Christians have shared in the last two thousand years. A sharing, simplicity of heart, and we are ready to face new combats.

1 January 1971

Two hours, passing from one group to another, from one individual to another. Immense variety of aspirations. Are we going to see an acceleration of the present atomizing process in the years to come? Those who are youngest give reasons for thinking so.

Understand, again and again understand, without being upset if some are rough in their language. Let go of certain mental structures. Universalize one's comprehension.

4 January

Three days of conversations with Italian workers involved in trade-union activities. Sergio analyses the Church's situation fiercely. I wonder whether he is going to say, as many do, that it is on the point of dying. But his conclusion is: 'The Church, dead? Oh no, the Church is continually moving forward'.

In his opinion, it is essential to criticize the Church's structures because that sets us free; it is a way of getting off our backs all that we cannot bear, in order to have room to live. Without such criticism the only way left would be to reject the Church globally. Conscientization and criticism help pass from simple refusal to creative initiatives.

Challenging passion for the Church, for the people of God, as found in this young trade-unionist, is very typical in a young Italian. How can we not discern in it a sign of love?

5 January

Two Christmas messages strike me particularly:

A card bearing a picture of Christ with a rifle. The greetings are full of friendship towards us but hard in their language: 'Men are not dogs, enough of that. We shall change things. Man no longer wolf for man. A challenge: hope and fight. Christ didn't rise for nothing. Meeting-place Taizé, Easter.'

And a letter from young Spaniards who form a small fraternal group. I find, on reading the heading of their writing paper, that they have given my name to their community. I immediately write to tell them not to.

7 January

The fire, constantly stoked during the day, is burning this evening on a bed of glowing embers. Beyond the windows snow sparkles, hardened by the frost. In my room Alain and I listen to the concerto in C minor for two harpsicords and orchestra by J. S. Bach. More than our words, certain passages of the concerto communicate a wealth of gladness. Over twenty years of the same unblemished trust . . .

8 *January*

Aware of all one's thoughts, afraid of none . . .

10 January

This Sunday is one of the few in the year without meetings. I was expecting to see nobody and, one after another, I have seen a whole series of unexpected visitors. One was a young South American. He bears in him a wealth of faith lived generation after generation. But he is also hesitant. Is he going to be the rich young man of the Gospel, generous but superficial, or the man who, in spite of everything, will commit himself irrevocably? At the door I repeat: seek Christ, not secondarily but as your first love and so, at once, as your essential joy. I sense in him the sadness of the man who longs. . . . Will he accomplish something?

15 January

Day of shadows. André Thurian is dying of a cancer. We are the same age. On the telephone, his aged mother, 85 years old: poor, broken voice in the twilight of her life.

And in the post a letter from Peter Rutishauser. He tells me the result of his operation: a cancerous tumour. All he asks for is a few more years to work.

Easier to consent to our own death than to that of those who are close to us. Rational explanations are of no help.

20 *January*

Visit to the stable. Our three cows are chewing the cud, indifferently. Only the goat lifts her head, intrigued. Visit to the little church. Return to the house. Down in the valley a frog is croaking, the first sign of coming spring.

22 *January*

Suppose that, because of the pressures of our consumer society we became so turned against it as to reject the discoveries of technical science? The civilization of technology is not at fault, being in itself a neutral value. The whole question is the use to which it is put. It can be a mighty force to set men free, offering the means to deliver them from subjection to the elements, floods, epidemics . . . it allows agriculture and medicine to advance . . . as never before.

Any form of civilization carries its threats. But whatever the civilization may be, Christ is there, close to man, and today he is close to man as he tries, with new knowledge, to reharmonize something of the creation.

POLITICAL COMMITMENT, STRUGGLE FOR MAN

Those most generous amongst today's youth tremble at the impossible privileges enjoyed by a fraction of mankind. In the Southern Hemisphere those most aware revolt brutally against the northern continents. In the Northern Hemisphere, the more affluence parents offer, the more irritated the children become, losing their tempers but champing in vain at the bit.

Bands of iron enclose us. Increasingly, a concern for security through material things is hastening the self-imprisonment of the consumer society in the Northern Hemisphere, as it grows daily richer. We are moving towards an ever greater imbalance: the northern continents, wallowing in material riches, secrete an economic and cultural system which maintains the southern continents in a state of subordination.

At the present moment, to refuse a commitment for man in order to live nothing more than closeness to Christ is to fall into a passive pietism, or individualism.

How could one say, 'Lord, Lord', but then not do the will of God? And part of that will is commitment in favour of man, victim of man. During the second world war many Christians in Europe prayed but remained oblivious to all that was happening around them, particularly in the extermination camps.

Today as earlier, our silences and our refusal to take risks can be ways of giving our support, consciously or unconsciously, to particular political regimes. In certain dramatic cases the silence of the Churches has been such as to amount to an almost explicit political commitment, going so far as to sanction oppression. In this domain we have a whole past history to digest and we are far from having come to an end with it.

But if some Christians, reacting against this passive pietism and the silence of the Churches, were to rush into extreme kinds of political options, only subsequently splashing the name of Jesus over their choice, it could be said that they in turn were hitching Christ to their wagon.

It is not possible for the Christian to set the cart before the horse. How can our whole existence be involved in a struggle among the oppressed, with the risk of losing our life through love, if we do not constantly draw on the Christian sources and find refreshment in them? It is then that, like God, man becomes creative. Pursuing within himself an adventure with the risen Lord, step by step, in an ardent struggle for greater justice, he takes his place in the march of man and mankind toward liberation from oppression.

23 January

Visit from the Anglican bishop Oliver Tomkins. He was the only priest present when the first brothers committed themselves for life in 1949. At today's meal we talked of the ground covered since, of our impressions.

He was also at Taizé for the inauguration of the church on 6 August 1962. Would we ever dream of inaugurating a building today? I would like to see our church sunk beneath the ground, buried in the depths, like a catacomb. Eight metres high, it already seems to date from another age.

During our meal, my eyes wandered over the country-side stretching beyond the windows of the room. The ploughed fields, studded with great sheets of standing water, glistened beneath the lowering sky. Certain twigs, red with the first rising sap, hinted that spring will soon burst through. Beside the clock, a vase of yellow jasmine, picked this morning.

26 January

Letter from a Christian of a neighbouring village: 'I want you to know how much we need you in our Maconnais vineyards. . .'. I note these words, because they are from our home ground, which for centuries past has been so stony.

28 January

At noon, Jean-Luc was playing a piece by Bach on the organ in the style of the Art of Fugue. In the permanent struggle that has to be fought for Christ's sake with men of clear-cut temperaments, such moments when no restraint remains are like a quenching dew.

Night has fallen. Every evening at this hour I glimpse the light shining at the window of the house where two women of prayer live, both of them elderly. No one will ever know all that their presence has signified. Today the window is in darkness. They must have gone away. An emptiness in the night.

1 February

This afternoon José lit the bread oven in the kitchen. After the evening prayer, it only took a few scraps of wood for me to kindle it again. Above the embers a dull flame licked up and slipped into the chimney. Later in the evening the oven was emitting the odour of the bundle of kindling placed there ready to be lit tomorrow morning.

2 February

Next door, two doves are cooing. We managed to find them late last night at Paul Deschaumes' farm. In a few moments I am going to carry them to the church for the celebration of the eucharist and I am eager to see everyone's surprise. This is the day when Mary presents the child in the temple, with the offering of any poor family : a pair of doves.

23 February

Shrove Tuesday. We have invited people from the neighbourhood to an evening meal. The older ones show a dignity which says much of the culture transmitted through centuries of farming life.

29 March

One year today since the announcement of the Council of Youth. This year we were not expecting very many more for Easter, but there are already over six thousand registrations. We are obliged to knock down part of the facade of the church so as to extend it by a huge circus tent. The rapid decision was not easily taken. What lies in wait will demand a suppleness and adaptability of which we have as yet no conception.

14 April

Encounter a group from Toulouse. Suddenly I recall a journey from Toulouse in the night. I think that it was in the winter of 1966. That evening, speaking in a gymnasium, I had been obliged to climb into the ring. In the night train, once alone, I kept repeating to myself: Roger, this evening must be the last; you must never again accept to speak to such crowds. But I was forgetting that our ways are set by an Other and often lead in directions that we would rather not follow.

24 April

Eight children, between ten and twelve years of age, have just arrived. They are children of miners at Montceau who managed to find somebody ready to drive them over. They will stay until Monday, helping in the reception. At each service they are there, kneeling in single file.

At home, on Fridays they go to the local church and pray, without anyone ever suggesting that they should.

Supposing the springtime of the Church were being offered in the faces of children and old people from whom nothing is expected? Suppose they have received the spirit of prophecy?

What these eight children have spontaneously undertaken is so unexpected! Talking with them, I was fascinated by their attitude, stamped with a kind of seriousness.

26 April

With several of my brothers I have been to visit Marcel Buisson, the priest of Culles-les-Roches. He is 85. His face, still smooth, beams with happiness. An electric lamp over the table lights the room. The shutters are half-closed: since a heart attack he cannot make the effort necessary to open them completely.

He relates: 'I became a priest very late. They were against ordaining me. I was sick with scruples. It was a real sickness, fearing sin in everything. I never knew joy. The priest by whom I came to the priesthood assured me that I might only know joy at the very last. So I wait.'

At the back of his room, in a recess, is a plank from a confessional. Would he accept, if some of us came to receive absolution at his hands? 'There are better priests', is his reply, giving names. And he adds, 'I have been forty years in this village, but nothing has happened'. He spoke like this when I came to see him before. Like so many other people he does not believe that what he achieves can have any impact.

29 April

Yesterday evening Jean-Luc and Thomas returned from Spain. In Avila they arrived, unannounced, at the Carmel. The sister at the gate welcomed them without surprise, firing as her first question, 'How is Brother Roger?' Every day without exception, their community prays for us. I understand how it is that we hold firm.

30 April

Every evening at present I am drawn towards the north, to see the last gleams of light, to make out dimly the long ridges of the hills dipping down beyond St Gengoux. It is 11 o'clock. Far away, many glimmering lights join in a dance. What is this, isolated as we are here in the midst of poor, practically unlit villages?

10 May

Gave *Ta fête soit sans fin* [*Festival*] to be printed. Of all the pages written day after day in the last two years, which to choose? With the last full-stop comes the question, 'Have I managed to say what I intended?' No. Then why write? A boundary always remains, beyond which we are left alone with ourselves, whether we be writing or speaking spontaneously.

13 May

Denis has an aged aunt who writes just after her eighty-fifth birthday, 'Very often I glimpse Christ, as you see somebody around the house, not really seeing him, and yet seeing him'. She lives quite alone in a farmhouse high in the Jura.

23 May

At table, Edouard Gafaringa, a young African pastor from Remera in Rwanda. A man of openness and friendship. I begin, 'You are here to see children'. A look of astonishment. 'Why, are we anything but children?' A burst of laughter. As we part, he tells of his longing to go and live, with his wife and family, with my brothers in Kigali.

30 May

A brother, back from a journey in a country whose name is best not mentioned, tells of all that is being prepared there for the Council of Youth. If we lived uniquely for the Christians of that land, existence would already have a sense for us.

4 June

Splendour of my room in the early working hours. A warm light, objects clearly defined, the coolness of the air scarcely warmed since the night. Man goes to the far ends of the earth in search of what is offered very close at hand.

12 June

Have welcomed at our table all the week, Massarou, a young Japanese. In order to become a Christian, he was first obliged to adopt the concepts and systems of thinking of the western world. That was what the missionaries intended. He only began to grasp the Gospel after he had freed himself of westernisms. Then I said, 'Preside at the table, take my place here, and make us welcome, we are your prodigal sons, we are westerners as your missionaries were'. Massarou began to preside with incredible joy and tact.

14 June

In the plane from Paris to New York, in response to an invitation from the American bishops of the Anglican Communion. Childlike happiness. How I have danced recently for joy at the thought of crossing the ocean! America: a dream in my childhood. Stories of my great-grandfather. Since then, an undying nostalgia for the wide open spaces, a land without frontiers.

15 June

Meeting with the bishops. They ask me to talk of authority in the Church, and also of the ministry of the Pope.

Whence comes this inner calm, this absence of timidity? Only ten years ago, I never used to dare to speak in public, even in the church at Taizé. I remember that in August 1962, during the inaugural days of our church, I did not pronounce a single word in public.

A UNIVERSAL PASTOR

As ecumenism has advanced, could it be that an evolution has been partially stifled, thanks to the conspiracy of silence that has been maintained around the ministry of the Pope? Will there ever be a possibility of moving forward ecumenically if no appeal is made to a pastoral ministry of unanimity, on a universal scale? And in a very concrete fashion, because we are men with ears to hear and eyes to see.

A man named John made me move towards these perspectives. John XXIII, by his ministry, opened my eyes to this way of universality. As contemporaries of his witness to Christ, we remain challenged by him.

During the last conversation that I had with John XXIII, not long before he died, I sensed how his prophetic ministry had been refused and that, with that refusal, a turning-point of ecumenism had been missed. He had reversed the Counter-Reformation situation partly when he declared publicly, 'We will not put history on trial, we will not ask who was wrong and who was right'. He had taken huge risks. At the Second Vatican Council, going against much advice, he had had no hesitation in inviting non-Catholics. He had asked forgiveness for the past. He was ready to go a long way. I realized his hurt on receiving in return, from non-Catholics, nothing but polite words. During that last conversation I understood that a prophet had been rejected, that ears had been stopped. From that moment on, ecumenism was sure to sink down into a system of parallel roads, each denomination pursuing its separate course in simple peaceful coexistence, and nothing more than that.

If it is true that every local community needs a pastor to renew the communion between people ever inclined to scatter, how can there be hope of a visible communion between all the Christians of the whole world without a universal pastor? Not at the top of a pyramid, not set at the head (the head of the Church is Christ), but at the heart.

As universal pastor, is the bishop of Rome leading us towards a Church of communion, not looking for support to any economic or political powers? If so, then he, borne up by his local Church, is going to count for much in the search to promote a communion between us all.

What things to ask of such a pastor, called to be a bishop in poverty? Surely, to expound the sources of faith for each generation, and in a very few words to invite Christians—and also many men beyond the Church's frontiers—to struggle against oppression and injustice.

Of course, the bishop of Rome is weighed down with an enormous burden of history, which at present still makes it hard for the specific features of his vocation to be discerned. Today he is called to rid himself of local pressures, in order to be as universal as he can be, in order to be free to tell out prophetic intuitions. And also to be free to exercise an ecumenical ministry by which to build up communion between all the churches, even calling upon those who refuse his ministry.

Perhaps the 'servant of God's servants' has a responsibility, not just for Catholics, but also for non-Catholics? In a word: to confirm his brothers, so that they may live by a single faith, a single mind. 'Peter, confirm your brothers'.

Maybe, by writing these lines I have wounded someone, hung a stone about his neck. Then let him hang that stone, too heavy for him, around my own neck. Not that I pretend to be able to bear it, but at least I shall try.

16 June

Even in New York, I lose none of my rural habits. At around four in the morning I jump out of bed to see what the weather is going to be. But the sky is still dark, whereas at Taizé, once three is past, it begins to take on colour and catches my breath with slow outbursts of new light.

At about six, I go along to the kitchen and find Beatrice, an old Brazilian woman, tiny and plump, walking with difficulty. Her existence is shot through with the harshest ordeals, humiliation and desertion. All her life long she has tried to give love.

17 June

Yesterday the gathering of bishops was impressive by its attentiveness. Whilst speaking, struck by their concentration, I included moments of silence. They are necessary; pauses to breathe in. But by them I also find that I can sense whether or not my words are really stimulating reflection. These silences taught me much. I had not known the quality of these Anglican bishops before. It is not for nothing that they are descendants of the pioneers who set out westwards.

In between our talks, I try to discover the futuristic side of New York. Nothing is more impressive than the great towering buildings. Disappointed at so much uniformity and monotony. And the youth is not so very different from that of Europe.

18 June

In the whole of my stay in New York, I did not speak a single word in English. Could it be because of a sentence that my father used to repeat in years past, 'You do not speak a foreign tongue in order to offend other persons' ears'?

But sitting beside the driver in a taxi, I dared tell him in English my joy on seeing in New York men and women gathered from the northern and southern continents. In spite of all the present conflicts, could there be here an anticipation of future humanity? He does not contradict me, I even sense in him a tacit agreement.

Now we are flying over Ireland. In the central aisle of the plane a young mother is standing with a tiny baby in her arms. The child's head, resting on its mother's shoulder, is rolling from side to side. In him, all the children of the whole world are present. His mother is tirelessly stroking his back, as though by that gesture she were giving him life.

As we left this morning, Beatrice was radiant. I had learned more of her history. Two years ago she was operated on for cancer. At that time she used to say, 'It is good that God has chosen me, because I know how to suffer'. As we parted, I kissed the hands of this old Brazilian cook, saying, 'I want to kiss the hands of a saint'. Her reply, 'Don't say that, it is a heresy, call me a missionary'. To which I answered, 'A saint is nothing other than a witness of Jesus Christ and you are that more than many, many others'. Her eyes filled with tears, her brow dark, almost black and marked by cobalt treatment. And I added, 'We shall pray together for the leaders of the Church, for them not to be afraid of the future any more, and even less afraid of young people'. I heard her reply, 'With young people, it is never any good pulling on the leash to make them change, the only thing that counts is goodness'.

27 June

A new family of Portuguese migrants has just arrived at Taizé: Antonio, his wife, their four youngest children, and their son-in-law Francisco. Two whole days by train. A final departure from their native land in order to come and settle here. Francisco returned ill from Angola. Twenty-four years old, he is gaunt as a skeleton. Soon he will be followed by his wife and children. We and these different families will live close to one another at Taizé. How can we achieve a relationship of sharing without paternalism? Since my journey last winter to Paços de Ferreira, their village, that question has been haunting me. For so many ·migrant workers, exile means a reduction of their humanity.

3 July

When I ask the children kneeling by my side whom we should pray for, this is a frequent reply: for Jesus, for God. As though they are so aware of the gratuitous that they consider all requests to be superfluous.

The seriousness of the three little Portuguese girls who arrived last week is a sign of their parents' situation. To help the family remain free towards us, I would like to be able to tell them to space out their visits to the church. But I fear that I might wound something in them. They alone know why they come to share in our common prayer.

7 July

A friend, a physicist, asked me recently: how do you manage to run so many meetings without administration or turnstiles? If he only knew the constant reviewing it demands. He also had this to say: as his authority increased and his audience grew, Christ troubled people in power, Jews and Romans. That, they could not forgive. So they panicked and set to work to provoke his failure. At such moments the masochists appear, 'Happy are they who are defeated'. They are pessimistic about any vaguely new burst of life.

16 July

The press hints at new relationships between the western powers and China. Alone in the wood, I sing.

26 July

Long conversations with a young South American bishop. He is going to spend the summer with us. What is to be feared in his country is not the imprisonment and torture of young Christians. Without knowing it, those responsible for these acts oblige the Christians to come to grips with their own identity and prevent them from identifying the Church with a political system. The problem lies in the Church. It lies in the uncontrollable loss of heart amongst young priests or young lay people, often the very best of them. They have gone as far as they could, and have finally left the Church for ever. 'I weep', he says. 'I weep whenever another weeps. I have inherited that from my father.' I interrupt, 'Without that inheritance, you would be completely overwhelmed and crushed'.

28 July

To a youth from Central America, I found myself once more insisting that I do not intend to give advice, that each of us has to find his way forward from his human poverty, that he must not look for a 'spirit of Taizé'. He replied, rather impetuously, not to say violently, 'It is already a spirit, not to want there to be one'.

4 August

At the end of the morning just thirty minutes remained to see seven different people.

Henri, a young French boy just back from Portugal, tells of a tense moment in his journey. He and his fiancée were almost killed when a munitions dump exploded. The town was full of terror, a grenade skimmed past his face. Then he gives me a sprig of olive that he had been given by a young Portuguese boy about to leave for the war in Angola, who explained, 'I shall never really be a soldier. My trade is looking after olive trees—the tree of peace. I have truly never thought of using a rifle. Today I leave for Africa. I am a man dressed as a soldier but remember that, whatever happens, I shall remain a human being.'

After Henri comes Helder, a boy of eighteen from Portugal. I invite him to come to lunch tomorrow with the other Portuguese: José, Antonio, Fernando, Manuel. What can we accomplish together?

I have to be quick. There are others to see. I can hear the laughter of a young couple waiting. But I remain absorbed by the thought of all those men dressed as soldiers, leaving their land for an impossible cause.

5 August

A meal with the five Portuguese. At once I reveal the question that is burning me. Thirty years ago there was the war, and I was living here surrounded by victims of Nazism. And I ask myself: Could I today be keeping the kind of silence that at that time I condemned in Christians who refused to adopt a clear stand? The meal was full of gravity for which I reproached myself. I would have liked there to have been a note of festivity. But to no avail.

6 August

Stanislas has returned! And in him all Africa, with its exuberant quickness of heart! Just before he set out for Europe he had an experience which I noted down as he was relating it. He went to visit a group of African sisters and as bishop, he was to receive the perpetual vows of a number of them. He asked if they really grasped all that celibacy entails. They made this reply: If the Church were to say that it no longer makes any sense to believe in the Risen Christ, then we would have nothing left but suicide: if Jesus Christ is not risen there is no point in committing our lives.

7 August

Telephone call from the Vatican. On Monday the *Osservatore Romano* will announce that 'henceforth there is to be a representative of the Prior of Taizé at the Holy See'.

I at once went out to walk in the garden. The night's heavy rain was steaming up, warmed by the sun-gorged earth.

Who are you in this event? I see myself, a poor man

walking on the wild grass. For the moment I cannot assess the extent of this agreement signed just three weeks ago. But one thing I know : I love that 'pilgrim Church that is at Rome' and its bishop. What can I ask of him? Surely, to give us light, to warm us with a fire, to stimulate communion among all the Churches?

8 *August*

About yesterday. I knew that it was coming. I thought that perhaps the demands which I expressed about the ministry of the Pope, at the conference of Pax Romana in July, would hold things up. But not at all. To have a representative close to the Pope : not that it means any lessening in the effort to find a more intense communion with the bishop of Rome.

9 *August*

Many exchanges, far into the evening. Grave situations, some without any apparent issue. As a result, I lie awake in the night. Impossible to digest so much human distress. Lying on my bed and lifting a corner of the curtain, I discover through my window the garden flooded with bright moonlight. I go out and walk along the hill as far as the hermitages. In the distance, at the heart of the night, Italians are singing. The air is poised, motionless.

10 *August*

An expert on China tells me how in Chinese the word 'crisis' is formed by two characters : one meaning catastrophe and the other hope.

11 August

In Northern Ireland a section of humanity, deprived of basic rights for centuries, feels that it is being deliberately oppressed. Recent events oblige us to ask what we could do to bring peace in such a prolonged conflict. But yesterday young Irish people repeated what others were saying a year ago, 'Do not come over for the moment. It is up to us to act for ourselves.'

15 August

After the midday meal, Dom Luis left us. We rose from the table and his eyes were brimming with tears. I, on the contrary, was holding my emotions in check, as I learned to do when a child. We never wept in the presence of other people. But once alone, who will ever know?

Luis would like us to spend two months living together in a Latin-American slum. But how can I tear myself away from here? Any prolonged absence means a return that is inhumanly overburdened. But since my five days in New York I am burning to cross the sea again.

16 August

Refused to see journalists and television reporters from various countries. Nobody can tackle too many things at once and to receive them at present would be an excessive burden. But it is not fair towards news-men and women who do their work with great honesty.

17 August

With the approach of the Council of Youth, I cannot bring myself to be worried—not even when certain people touch on the great difficulties involved. I trust the intuitions of the young people from so many different lands who gather here, return home to search and pray, come back here again. In these hot August nights, there are evenings when I find myself out walking beneath a sky heavy with stars, at the same time as thousands of young people are camping on the hill. And I tell myself: the innumerable intuitions of these young people are like points of light in my night. As yet nothing is perceptible, and still my night is festive, aflame and full of an immense hope. The future, young people—the two are one. No, I am not anxious about the future. A springtime of the Church is at the door. Very soon, it will be a fire giving us warmth.

18 August

A blow-fly is buzzing in the thick midday heat. In a gust of joy my childhood leaps up. I listen to the other noises, light and distant: the trickle of water flowing into the trough, a man's footsteps on the path. The dry-stone wall sheltering the garden is bursting with well-being beneath the clinging vines.

19 August

Dreamed that the house in which I was born was in flames. I should be left with another, less loved. I felt shocked and hurt. I comforted myself with the thought that an insurance policy would pay for the furnishings, but the letters were going to vanish for ever. . . .

24 August

Visit from a foreign bishop. I wanted to hear what he had to say, but his young vicar-general kept bombarding me with ideas and questions. As he arrived, he had been anxious to let me hear some not very kind words spoken by a pastor—competitive ecumenism at its worst. Shaken, I try to turn to other subjects. No good. Twice, in an attempt to reply to his indiscreet questions I give him texts to read. But he only continues, the bishop still saying nothing. To finish with, I invite my visitors to read the texts in silence and I put on a record of Valentini's trumpet concerto in C major. It is the first time that I have had recourse to this method as a way of putting an end to such nonsense.

26 August

Wrote to Michel, at Recife, 'If the pen were to express our communion I would need to write to you in letters of flame'. In the midst of all the contradictions in which we are set by our vocation, this brother's courage bears me forward.

27 August

At this moment of the afternoon, a beam of sunlight is dropping through the half-open shutters and flooding the two pages of the atlas open on the regions of the north of Siberia and Sweden. In these vast polar lands, the heat is coming to an end and the mosquitos are gorging themselves with blood before a rapidly approaching death.

Here, lingering of high summer.
Still I will sing

maturity of life,
the swollen chestnuts,
the splendid gentle warmth of night,
the odour of leaves that fall too soon,
grass drenched with heavy dew,
soil's thirst quenched.

7 September

The day before yesterday, Grégoire and Jean-François returned from Sotto il Monte accompanied by Giuseppe Roncalli. Now that he is aged, he is very like his brother, John XXIII. Fulgenzio, his grandson, is there too. I had already noticed last year his solid maturity. He is only twenty.

Giuseppe Roncalli talks of his childhood, that of John XXIII. Their aged uncle owned a total of seven books; it was he who used to tell them about the Gospel. Winter and summer alike, all went to Mass at 5.30 every morning. Then in the evening, the family would pray together.

When he was Nuncio, the future John XXIII used to help out his family. They had only a few cows and one day a cow died. He wrote, 'The money I am sending is for sugar and oil. I cannot do more. I bless the cows, even the one that died'.

Then Giuseppe Roncalli told of his first visit to his brother once he was Pope. The two brothers are discussing how certain Christians live in great wealth. The Pope says, 'I always remind them to think of what happens in the Gospel to those who are rich'. Like the old Bergamasque peasant that he is, Giuseppe Roncalli often refers to the god Mammon—money. He notes that the young people here live poorly and tells Fulgenzio, 'From here will emerge something that my brother began'.

THE SPUR OF MARXISM. . . ?

*Two things I ask of thee, Lord, deny them not to me
before I die: Remove far from me falsehood and lying;
and give me neither poverty nor riches. Feed me with
the food that is needful for me. In abundance, I might
deny thee and say, 'Who is the Lord?' Wretched, I
might steal and profane the name of God*

*(Words prayed by a believer, five centuries before
Christ)*

*Feed me with the food that is needful for me. Yes, the
food that is needful. Not misery. Not pretended poverty,
puritan austerity. And not riches either. Twenty-five
centuries ago, this believer in God had already sensed that,
with his security coming from accumulated wealth, he
would be bound to doubt in God and say, 'The Lord does
not exist!'*

The long history of Christians is full of a host of in-
consistencies. Far from continuing the 'socialization'
which was a reality in the early Church, Christians have
hoarded wealth. Since the sixteenth century they have
given their approval to a system of money-lending with
interest, until then forbidden; in the Middle Ages those
practising it were excommunicated. And Christians have
also consented to work being organized in society in such
a manner that profits are not redistributed to all but kept
back to benefit a tiny number.

In the Churches today, vast sums of money are tied-up.
In certain northern European countries immense regions
of forest constitute an inalienable patrimony of the
Church. In certain other lands, the State, by a system of
church-taxes, pours a mint of money each year into the
Church's accounts. Elsewhere . . .

And it is not uncommon to find Christians denouncing this state of things in the Churches but accumulating personal property for themselves. But the whole people of God is concerned, both clergy and laity. All together form a body, that unique communion called the Church.

Did the spur of Marxism have to be jabbed into the flesh of the people of God for them to be forced out of their sleep, woken up and driven to become a community of sharing, in solidarity with oppressed man? As though this spur was needed to make the people of God remember, by seeing a secularized expression of it, that the early Church practised a real community of goods?

Today's search involves demanding an end to all the failures to be consistent! But it does not mean moving off and forming small, purist congregations to deliver inflexible condemnations from puritan heights. As soon as man sets himself on the outside to condemn those within, he empties himself of all power of creativity, to say nothing of the human tenderness vital for whoever tries to follow Christ.

To be a living stone in the people of God, when it comes to the uses Christians make of wealth, is not a matter of passing irrevocable sentences on other Christians. It is a case of searching with them, in time and out of time, and hastening across the whole face of the earth if necessary, so as to exhort, persuade, beseech, set everything in movement without a break in communion . . . ready to weep alone when all one obtains is to be heard, but not listened to.

8 September

One question has kept coming up this summer: 'How are we to continue, once away from Taizé?' And I would reply: Nobody can possibly grasp all that there is in the Gospel. But if during your stay here you have understood just one word, just one gesture—almost nothing—then put that word, that gesture into your life, at once and intensively. When you have put one foot forward, that step will lead you on to other steps. Put into life the little that we have understood, and create on the basis of that tiny intuition, on the basis of our individual poverty. Strive to find just one intuition and then to live by it.

29 September

A question from Jacqueline: 'How are we to reconcile inner silence and contemplation with being politically involved alongside movements which see violence as a means of action?'

30 September

To an Argentinian visitor I was saying: as I listen to so many young political activists, it is mainly the left ear that has work, but the right is not completely idle!

1 October

Certain mental structures formed in childhood remain for ever, and around them all the events of life weave and reweave themselves.

On memory of mine. When I was about eight, I fetched from the attic all the best-bound volumes, including

Diderot's *Encyclopedia*. My mother was not very happy to see me organizing a whole library of old, dusty books in my room. But my father advised her, 'Let him be; a happy childhood marks a whole life'.

2 October

Bicycle ride with Robert. Both of us were surprised on discovering, ten minutes away from the house, a peaceful river, the Grosne, snaking quietly between oak trees. We continued on foot as far as the bridge at Cortemblin. On our left, a red sun was dipping into far-off mist, on our right a great moon already high in the heavens. The unfamiliar meanderings of the Grosne forced us in every direction. All my life I have longed for such landscapes; they lie at our door and I had not realized it.

6 October

Today I have only this to write: if so much pain is for Christ, for his body the Church, and for men, then I will continue.

15 October

This morning, something unique. In one long line, all the Carmelite sisters from Chalon were present at our prayer. They were leaving for ever the convent in which their community has lived for the past three centuries and were on the way to their new home not far from us. At the end of the prayer, I gave them a few nuts with the words:

These nuts were brought from Avila this spring and they come from a tree that tradition says was planted by St Theresa. Tradition and poetry coincide. Tradition knits an expression of continuity, with many kinds of threads, some sombre and some bright. So long as it does not grow hard, the resulting tissue can go on developing indefinitely, always covered with new designs.

16 October

Mrs Gandhi replies in a rather frustrating way: 'It is kind of you to offer to send volunteers to work in the refugee camps. But I feel that they can contribute more by mobilizing public opinion in their own countries.'

Always the same refusal of the north by the south. Make those around you more aware. We agree completely, even if that takes us a long way, or even to prison, as one of my brothers was saying. But communion cannot be just restricted to that.

19 October

Went to visit Francisco this morning. Always the same pale emaciated face. He is afraid that he is not getting any better. The oldest of his children, Martinho, is standing near his bed. And his wife is close by, with another child in her arms. Through the window I can see young people coming and going on the open space near the bells. They never suspect that in the same house as they come to on arriving, upstairs, there is a couple of Portuguese emigrants with many burdens to bear.

21 October

For weeks past, every morning I open the curtains to the same thrill. Hot light bounding from the ground in crystal greys. Beneath the lime trees and the maples stretch carpets of leaves. From time to time a slight mist rises from the valley and fills the sky, then these layers of leaves begin to sparkle.

22 October

A letter from Jean-Gérard, in the heart of black Africa:

Yesterday I saw a friend I have known since January. I was out on the road when I first met him, uneducated and poorest of the poor. Afterwards, he came to see me. He was looking for work. Now he often comes and tells me about his family and his friends. I have done nothing for him, except listen to what he says. Then the other day I told him that I would soon have to return to France, on which he said these words: 'I was a man with nothing, I did not have life. You listened to me. You gave me life and God. In Europe everyone is rich, there you will have no poor to be the friend of.'

26 October

Some underrate themselves, others push themselves forward: both attitudes come from the same narcissism, that throwback into childishness which prevents a man being himself.

30 October

Since last evening, I have been reflecting with Eugene Carson Blake, the General Secretary of the World Council of Churches. Towards the end of our exchanges he affirms: 'All my life I have been involved in running church institutions. I have always known what had to be said or done. In today's situation, I do not know any more.' I ask him 'Can I repeat to the young people in the Church this evening what you have just said?' He agrees. But I shall add this: it is when we are in the heart of a desert that we can expect a prophetic word.

8 November

Much hesitated whether to go to Paris in response to an invitation from Mrs Gandhi. I found it better for a brother to go with a message. That is not my place. Why? I cannot exactly explain it to myself ... traces of puritanism ... an embarassment in the presence of those with political responsibilities . . . and yet this woman, in the present drama of Bangladesh, inspires sympathy.

10 November

Often, especially since the announcement of the Council of Youth, I have heard how certain priests or pastors experience a sense of frustration on seeing so many young people coming on to the hill here, whilst their churches are emptying. Occasionally their pain turns into bitterness. Some even go so far as to publish articles designed to misrepresent the young who gather here and what they live while they are together. I have just been talking with one such person here in my room. . . .

13 November

A long interview for the Canadian television. The camera-man, already aging, has been here before; between us there exists a kind of complicity. The reporter, distrustful towards the Church without being aggressive, asks questions that are pertinent and honest. I give replies that I had not intended to give:

All of us in the West have inherited a mentality marked by the legalism and imperialism of ancient Rome, even though we may reckon ourselves freed from them. The Churches of the Reformation believed that they were ridding themselves of legalism and have simply produced a new kind. Certain Marxist lands denounce imperialism and organize another form of it, just as effective.

Employ much energy to change the structures of the Church? If it is simply to create new ones, what is the point? There exist other ways of advancing.

15 November

Spent an hour in Daniel's pottery. I enter with the attentiveness one always brings to places consecrated by ardent workmanship.

On a blackboard: figures, diagrams, mathematical equations. Hooked on to a plank are little coloured plaques, specimens of glaze with a formula written above each.

Systematic research leading to the creation of glazes based on minerals or plants found locally, using ashes from straw, reeds, ferns, acacias, oak branches. . . . Lengthy preparation before ever beginning to work up the lump of clay. A whole series of processes before each object is entrusted to the glow of the flames, finally to emerge bright and fascinating by its forms.

We talk together . . . I have the impression that I surprise Daniel when I say spontaneously: I find old people and children set me most at my ease. If I have come to be so attentive to the young, it is perhaps because I have heard so many of them tell me of the fog they are passing through. .

17 November

More and more I come to say to young men and women, about to leave here for distant homes: in monastic communities of women there are women practised in the exercise of discernment, often through many years of experience. Go and seek, in exchanges with one of them, to be understood as you are.

In times past, in masculine communities, if it was recognized that some had a charism, a great capacity for listening and intuition, then they were called to give the freedom of forgiveness, whether they were priests or laymen (in Eastern Orthodoxy, the *staretz*).

The same gifts exist in certain women living the common life. Why have people never recognized a similar feminine vocation of listening and intuition to convey forgiveness?

24 November

Rolling in the train towards Rome, I realize that the most vital hours of the past days were not those that I thought —the two evening meetings in churches packed with young people at Turin and Bologna.

The essential lies in this morning's encounter with a number of theological students. I searched their faces and in some I could sense scepticism, although accompanied by the desire to give their whole lives. We are in a civilization of criticism, but criticism supposes learning and also knowledge of oneself; otherwise it is nothing more than a continual projecting of one's own inner devastation on to others and the whole people of God.

26 November

We have been in Rome for two days. After so many stays here, I can measure the long distance covered, more often painful than easy. Why have I been so determined to persevere, when everything encouraged me to stay in Taizé? Why have I been so convinced of the necessity of these conversations here in Rome? I have been driven to pursue them, irresistibly, as though moved by a force coming from outside of myself.

28 November

First Sunday in Advent. There is a sea air blowing over the city. Yesterday, we walked until we were stiff. Today too, I was intending to walk but young people have recognized us in the street, so we must start inviting them to the house.

For several hours past a breeze has been blowing through the open window into my room. That is no substitute for the beam of sunlight which, at Taizé, shines on to the great wood planks of the floor. Here my room, giving on to the courtyard, is in perpetual twilight.

30 November

Coming home this evening with Max, we penetrated for a second to the far end of the courtyard of the Villa

Laetitia Bonaparte. From there we looked out on the criss-crossing lights of the passing cars. A confused hubbub reaches us at the back of the courtyard and through the high gateway the Piazza Venezia advances, recoils, dances.

3 December

Long private conversation with Paul VI. The mystic in him prevails. He longs to grasp the plan of God. When I talk to him of the young, he understands well. From his lips, never a word of warning.

At the close of our conversation, I say words which I had not intended to pronounce: 'The name of Taizé is heavy for us to bear, there are days when I long to see it vanish.' The Pope replies, 'No, the name of Taizé cannot disappear.' And he makes a generous parallel with another example in history. Paul VI goes on to add, 'The first time that we met, you told me that you were pilgrims on the move, and I have always remembered that'. That must have been when we talked together in 1949. True, we are pilgrims, our means are poor. And the Pope concludes 'I too am poor.'

8 December

Walk through the old medieval streets. Inner courtyards, hidden at the end of rundown alley-ways, beckon. We enter one. A fountain is trickling into an Etruscan coffin. A wall carpeted with greenery. Great pots overflowing with camellias. Above our heads, hanging galleries held up by goodness knows what, all is so decrepit. Washing hung in the windows.

Reaching the Via Giulia, we glimpse a green garden beyond an open gate. We enter briskly and find, set against the hills rising beyond the Tiber, a mandarine grove. Two girls are picking an abundant crop, in the depth of European winter.

11 December

The texts of the recent synod have just been made public. At the end of a long day, I have addressed a message to Paul VI to tell him especially:

> Celibacy—folly of the Gospel for men and proclamation of the coming Kingdom, will stimulate the Church in its unique vocation to be the salt of the earth. Celibacy is certainly not an easy option, it is a way by which men and women give their whole lives to Christ without keeping back part for the future. Because of it they receive a hundredfold, but with persecutions, experienced as an inner struggle for those entrusted to them by God. Far from being a contradiction of Christian marriage, celibacy will encourage Christians to discover the specific calling of the laity—a 'royal priesthood' set in each Christian which involves living Christ for men. Thus Christians will bear more explicitly than before a share in the common ministry of the Church.

12 December

Without restricting anything of the force of the call to celibacy, yesterday's synodical text does not exclude the possibility that the priesthood may be conferred on married men.

In recent months, I was unable to reconcile myself with the idea that the synod might abolish completely the link between priesthood and celibacy. I have been preparing myself to consent. But the anxiety at times was proportionate to the question: does the Catholic Church realize the radical reversal of values inherent in this? The celibacy of priests, folly of the Gospel, has maintained in the heart of the Church a mystical vein: the Church is ever led towards the invisible, the mystery of Christ, the irrational element of the Gospel. The marriage of priests would be a move towards the simply functional, the instrumental.

That it is necessary, in certain local situations, to ordain married men is something I am convinced of. But important that such men should first have proved themselves in married life, so as to avoid a future crisis in their ministry with their children in disagreement or in open revolt, or because their life's partner is unable to continue living imprisoned in an ecclesiastical set-up.

The marriage of priests will not resolve anything of the present crisis, which has nothing to do with marriage or celibacy. The collapse in the number of vocations is just as great in the protestant theological faculties, whose students have always been free to marry. As for the lack of maturity of the affections, that is something existing in single men as in those married.

The brutal and accelerating decline in vocations has its cause elsewhere, and demands infinitely more basic transformations.

13 December

Have been continuing yesterday's reflection about priesthood and laity.

As far as priesthood is concerned, although it may mean having few priests, it is important to change completely the way of preparing men for the ministry. Their preparation should communicate an ability to ask questions about one's existence all through life—to discover the why and then the why of the why of one's behaviour. Studies which are therefore more a period of bringing one's self into being than an accumulation of things written in books. In the future, knowledge will be acquired more and more in successive stages, all through life. The vital thing is to find the permeability that will enable us to welcome the rapid succession of waves which is going to pass across the human consciousness. All of this is also true for schools and universities in general.

As for the laity, how to make Christians discover the share of the common ministry set in each one? Faced with a lack of priests, lay people will be obliged to take their share—immense and almost unexplored—in a ministry that until now has been exercised almost solely by the clergy. The result will be a new complementarity between lay people and priests.

22 December

Return to Taizé. I am obliged to recognize the use to which my message to Paul VI has been put. A few sentences of it were published in the French press. Based on this, a denominational press-agency has published a commentary without quoting the terms I actually used—which distorts the sense of the text. Should I in turn reply in the press? No. All my life, when I have been attacked, I have striven within myself to maintain silence.

23 December

This evening I read a letter from a young couple. Knowing their positions, I expected to find them writing reproachfully about the message of Paul VI, which has earned me so many letters of protest. But instead, they announce the birth of a child . . .

26 December

Some young women tell me that they have not succeeded in their attempt to live together in community.

Success is a social notion standing poles apart from the Gospel. To aim to succeed begets a subtle form of self-centredness. Accept that we always stumble. Our expressions are awkward, never perfect. Our symbols are ambiguous.

27 December

The application of ecumenism at present sets us on the horns of a dilemma: how to enter into a universal communion without asking any people to deny the belief transmitted to them in all honesty by their forefathers? As a temporary solution, for the generation of the present turning-point, shall we be able to find a possibility of 'double allegiance'?

31 December

In the sky a few pale stars, deep night and hard frost.

Have once more closed the door, my room with its silence holds me. I have too much loved with my whole being for solitude to become a matter of course.

Age gains ground little by little. To everything consent is given. The years have set checks on the boiling flood. At last I know how to love. Within me, the ceaseless streams of love that spring up at every moment flow quietly between banks rising in the midst of wide stretching plains. No trace of bitterness. Not that the fire is extinguished. It will keep burning on until the chill of death.

At present nothing appals me, neither life nor death. Expectation of unending rest for the flesh and the blood . . . So then, one winter's night, let that gentle rest come and with it life that has no end.

THE SILENCE OF CONTEMPLATION

Prayer, descending into the depths of God, is not there to make life easy for us. Prayer: not for any kind of result, but in order to create with Christ a communion in which we are free.

When man strives to give expression to this communion in words, we have conscious prayers. But our understanding can only deal with the outer surface of ourselves. Very soon it comes up short . . . and silence remains, to such an extent as to seem a sign of the absence of God.

Instead of coming to a standstill with the barrenness of silence, know that it opens towards unheard-of possibilities of creation: in the underlying world of the human person, in what lies beyond our consciousness, Christ prays, more than we can imagine. Compared with the vastness of this secret prayer of Christ in us, our explicit praying dwindles to almost nothing.

Certainly, the essence of prayer takes place above all in great silence . . .

All prayer remains arduous for any who are left to themselves. God has made man a social being, and has given him a 'political' calling. Perhaps this is why contemplation becomes less of an effort when it is lived in fellowship with others?

The silence of contemplation! Within each of us lie unknown gulfs of doubt, violence, secret distress . . . and also chasms of guilt, of things unacknowledged, so that gaping below our feet we sense an immense void. Our impulses seethe; we do not know their origin; perhaps they come from some ancestral or genetic memory. So let Christ pray in us, trusting as a child, and one day these gulfs will be inhabited.

One day, later on, we shall discover that there has been a revolution in ourselves.

With time, contemplation begets a happiness. And that happiness, proper to free men, is the drive behind our struggle for and with all people. It is courage, energy to take risks. It is overflowing gladness.

5 January 1972

Resume this journal. Nothing can replace writing it, the slow reflecting, worked-out on the shining paper, under the lamp, in rounded characters.

7 January

In days of darkness, when I am obliged to face up to a reality which even involves acts of repressive violence, I like to remember what John XXIII said: 'Be joyful, seek the best and let the sparrows chirp.'

It is two in the morning. In the garden, the mildness of a spring night. Sat for a few minutes out on the porch, from where I could see through the window into the *salle claire*. Its pine floor was warm with tints of lemon.

14 January

Yesterday, I asked little Jean-Paul whom we should pray for: 'For all the people of the world.'

So strong a sense of the universal in such a young child! True, for two thousand years past we have sung our unbelievable hope in a Christ come to set every human being free—not only those who explicitly draw their life from him, but every man in every place, not a few privileged people or a single ethnic group, but all men, of every race and people.

20 January

At times, people of my generation find themselves seized in the jaws of a vice: between explanations demanded by the old, weary Church, and the aspirations of the rising generations. Reject neither.

22 January

A letter in the mail that counts for much. It is from an old peasant woman. I am going to copy a few lines here. When I come to choose passages from this journal to publish, I wonder if I shall dare let these lines past?

> I am making a fool of myself by writing to you. Who am I, a poor peasant, to write to Brother Roger? But all the same, I want to say thank you . . . especially for *Festival*. In that book, a friend is talking to me of the Friend in words I feel but cannot express. Thank you for your optimism, your confidence in man. And for the poetry, youthful and fresh in spite of all the difficulties. I gladly reply to say that we are both of us shaped by the same mould.

10 February

Went walking with Clément in the vineyards at Saules. Red soil. Vast horizons ending, above the Jura, in a long bank of clouds. Such outings are refreshing. This brother, with his joy at being alive, his peals of laughter . . .

16 February

With Christians split into innumerable denominations, it is easy to keep finding new reasons for remaining fixed on parallel tracks which, by definition, will never come together. But in the end this becomes a way of avoiding the question, even to the point of betraying the ecumenical expectancy of the people of God.

18 February

We have had Catholic brothers for several years now, forming at home here together a single community, and this has allowed us to discover a way of creating: when Christians set out really to live together, they soon discover their common faith.

19 February

A lengthy letter from Hector. The struggle in which he is involved with poor peasants in Colombia is a hard one. Having too many things to do this morning, I left part of his letter to read during the afternoon. There, he tells me that Bishop Valencia has been killed in an accident. This man, of a great openness that many found incomprehensible, was a point of reference for many young Colombians, Christians and even non-Christian revolutionaries.

After prayer this evening, we were together to welcome a new brother into the community. I would have liked to have spoken of this bishop's death. Who is going to fill the void left in the lives of so many young Colombians fighting for greater justice? That question was so strong in me that my voice would not work. Impossible to utter three words. I had to cut short our council.

20 February

Yesterday my mother was saying to a friend: 'I talk to God, we understand each other. I pray for everybody. On days when I am too weak for that, God understands too.' A few days ago she said to Ghislain: 'What counts for God is the heart.'

27 February

Arrived yesterday at Barcelona, invited by the Abbot of Montserrat who was in Taizé last year. On Friday, passing through Perpignan, I was eager to make acquaintance with Madame Durocher, the grandmother of one of my brothers.

We found the narrow street in which she lives as night was falling. I spot a woman with white hair arranged in a bun; seeing in her features a similarity with those of her grandson I embrace her spontaneously, in the middle of the street!

We climb up to a small dark room. Out of breath from the stairs, she gradually recovers her voice and it becomes melodious. She announces that their parish priest, and the bishop, want to come to greet me. I try to defend myself. I am here for her, to hear what she has to say. The little I have already grasped suggests how great a quality of intuition lives within her.

Here on the first floor I glimpse in the gloom a terrace. Greenery at this height? She leads me out on to it. 'Here is where I spend the summer.' The palm tree in the centre of the tiny garden is the highest in the town. There are flower beds nestling in thick foliage. I breathe in the perfume of this corner of earth at the heart of an old city. In a flash I imagine her, all through the summer, hidden here: Fulfilment in solitude.

After the meal she talks about her husband. One image follows another. One Christmas, in Provence at the end of the war, they had almost nothing to eat. In spite of her husband's reticence, she went and bought a kilo of sugar on the black market to make some sweets. The words weave together, mistletoe and pale honey ...

It is getting late. In spite of protests, Robert, Patrick, and

I continue our journey and only stop to sleep once we are beyond the Spanish border.

28 February

Yesterday we were walking along a path with a view of the buildings of Montserrat perched between two steep peaks.

Our Christian life is also set between two mountains! There is that of the transfiguration, Christ making use of all that lies within man and transforming it—the good and the not-so-good, hatred and love . . . and the mountain on which Jesus knew temptation. So attractive, the one who there offered him domination over all the kingdoms of the earth . . .

4 March

I have pinned to my wall a photograph of Chou-en-Lai, cut out of a Spanish newspaper. The statesman is lifting his hand in greeting as Nixon is about to leave China. Over the face of this aging intellectual spreads an inexpressible suffering.

18 March

Pierre-Yves was speaking of that voice that doubts and mutters within us, 'O yes, God chooses such and such, but I have nothing to make him consider me, my prayer is never more than a projection of myself.' To which Pierre-Yves was remarking: is that humility, really? It is almost, and yet it is just the opposite. It is simply a form of exaggerated love of self, a love turned into hatred. Now self-hate is closer to pride than to humility. If we refuse to believe, even just a little, in our love for God, we shall be unable to believe in his love for us.

23 March

If at present certain Christian institutions are breaking down all over the world, is that not, in the end, all to the good for the Churches . . . perhaps for a communion?

24 March

A young couple from Argentina inform me that they have decided to live in community with other couples. I ask them if they are ready for such a plan to remain provisional. I know that any family, however open and generous the parents may be, is bound to condition its members. But is their plan not going to submit their children to too many pressures?

We are asking the same questions with several couples who are thinking of coming to live near us on the hill.

25 March

A few months ago we learned that, unknown to us, a group of capitalists had formed a company with the aim of setting up a motel, a luxury hotel, and a holiday village not far from Taizé. Certain business-men had been persuaded that here was an opportunity not to be missed. Relief today on learning that their plans have misfired.

26 March

Dreamed last night in poetry. A child, I am with my sisters. In bright morning light, we are climbing along a wide driveway, covered by high, thick greenery. In the foliage bright-coloured birds are flitting. A splendid green bird with gleaming plumage comes swooping down beside me. At the top of the drive, the horizon opens onto wild expanses of countryside. On the road is a shop. We stop. I fill a wicker basket with all kinds of things, toys and other presents.

27 March

Monday in Holy Week. The readings of the Passion fall into ground stirred up by recent events. With many young people, here and far away, we have allowed the desert soil of our persons to be ploughed over. Many have met together, in the farthest corners of the world. So many discoveries, a wealth of friendship and mutual trust.

But shadows too have been discovered. In recent months we have been submitted to almost unbearable pressures. We have found that there exists a visceral fear of youth. And a fear that here we pay too much attention to those who are young. I have so often heard people say, 'These young people are going to lead you by the nose'.

No real adventure can be lived together without temptation appearing. The tempter offered Christ all the kingdoms of the world if he would only submit to him. These kingdoms have names: the very illusory search to gain influence over others, the desire for power. Invariably the result is sterility.

If we ignore these rearguard combats, what remains is a great dynamism that can carry us far, very far.

28 March

In all the current mutations of human behaviour there is one constant: the need to live instantaneously, whence a lack of attention for history. Yet man is always linked to a past, recent or distant, that no break can ever really abolish. Ancestral memory? Genetic memory? Who can decide?

2 April

Easter morning. After the eucharist, the crowds coming to give me the Easter greeting were so great that I had to laugh to myself at my limits. I found a gesture: I would lay on my shoulder for a second the head of each person as they passed in an unbroken stream. Some would say a few words, sometimes something grave. In two hours, so many faces!

3 April

God! Too dazzling to be seen, God is a God who blinds our eyes. Christ restrains the consuming fire and lets God appear without splendour.

Be he recognized or unknown, Christ is there, close to each one. He is present in secret, light in our darkness, burning man's heart. He is so united with man that he dwells in him, even though he may not know it.

But Christ is also, as God, quite other than ourselves. He exists in himself, could exist without man. He is the object of man's untiring search to see him face to face. He stands ahead of the human person, beyond us.

The day will rise when in him will come fulfilment for all created worlds, worlds perhaps inhabited by other beings made in the image of God. If beyond our present perceptions, a new dimension of communion should be discovered, its source would be bound to lie in Christ. The body of Christ, his Church, can only conform more and more to the dimension of the whole creation.

4 April

Of all that has happened in the past few days, what is most vital? Of course, sixteen thousand here together. Of course, the announcement that the Council of Youth will open in 1974. But above all the common prayer. During these Easter days, it has carried everything, like a ship ploughing through a foaming sea. It has borne us forward in spite of the burden of tensions and struggles, be they caused by immediate problems or by obstacles lying ahead. Creating as free men, we know the object of our search. Nothing to fear.

RELIGION $2.95

Struggle and Contemplation

Brother Roger, Prior of Taizé

In this book Brother Roger continues the personal journal begun in *Festival* (The Seabury Press, 1974) with reflections from the years 1970-1972. Against the background of preparations for the World Council of Youth we see him struggling to reconcile the call to political commitment with the central place of silence, listening, and prayer in his life.

A Crossroad Book
The Seabury Press • New York

ISBN: 0-8164-2106-4